A
Literature Unit
for

The Incredible Journey

by Sheila Burnford

Written by Jane S. Pryne

Teacher Created Materials, Inc.
P.O. Box 1040
Huntington Beach, CA 92647
©1995 Teacher Created Materials, Inc.
Made in U.S.A.

ISBN 1-55734-521-X

Edited by Janet Cain

Illustrated by Kris Sexton

Cover Art by Nancee McClure

Table of Contents

Introduction

A book with an adventure-filled story can transport us to new places that we have never experienced before. Our imaginations allow us to make these incredible journeys without ever leaving the safety of our community. Consequently, a book can become a priceless treasure that enriches our lives forever.

In *Literature Units*, great care has been taken to select books that are sure to become good friends!

Teachers who use this unit will find the following features to supplement their own valuable ideas.

- Sample Lesson Plan
- Pre-reading Activities
- Biographical Sketch and Picture of the Author
- Book Summary
- Vocabulary Lists and Suggested Vocabulary Activities
- Chapters grouped for study, with each section including:
  — quizzes
  — hands-on projects
  — cooperative learning activities
  — cross-curriculum connections
  — extensions into the reader's own life
- Post-reading Activities
- Two Culminating Activities
- Three Different Options for Unit Tests
- Bibliography
- Answer Key

We encourage you to use this unit as part of your teaching strategies and hope that your students will find this book to be a unique treasure.

Sample Lesson Plan

Each of the lessons suggested below can take from one to several days to complete.

LESSON 1

Introduce and complete some or all of the pre-reading activities found on page 5.

Read "About the Author" with your students. (page 6)

Introduce the vocabulary list for Section 1. (page 8)

LESSON 2

Read Chapters 1-2. As you read, place the vocabulary words in the context of the story and discuss their meanings.

Choose a vocabulary activity. (page 9)

Label a map of Canada. (page 11)

Make a chart about industry. (page 12)

Research glaciers and make a travel brochure describing glaciers of interest. (page 13)

Make a list of ways to live with situations beyond our control. (page 14)

Administer the Section 1 quiz. (page 10)

Introduce the vocabulary list for Section 2. (page 8)

LESSON 3

Read Chapters 3-4. Place the vocabulary words in context and discuss their meanings.

Choose a vocabulary activity. (page 9)

Collect data and organize it on two graphs. (page 16)

Do research to learn about local Native American tribes. (page 17)

Learn about imagery. (page 18)

List ways to care for a pet and write a paragraph persuading others to care for their pets. (page 19)

Administer the Section 2 quiz. (page 15)

Introduce the vocabulary list for Section 3. (page 8)

LESSON 4

Read Chapters 5-6. Place the vocabulary words in context and discuss their meanings.

Choose a vocabulary activity. (page 9)

Make a model of a beaver's lodge and dam using a diagram. (page 21)

Identify character traits. (page 22)

Predict a new outcome for a story event. (page 23)

Write a new chapter for the novel. (page 24)

Administer the Section 3 quiz. (page 20)

Introduce the vocabulary list for Section 4. (page 8)

LESSON 5

Read Chapters 7-9. Place the vocabulary words in context and discuss their meanings.

Choose a vocabulary activity. (page 9)

Research porcupines, and make a model of one. (page 26)

Make a word search using the names of Canadian animals (page 27)

Use a metric scale to determine distance on a map. (page 28)

Identify ways to use, but preserve the environment. (page 29)

Administer the Section 4 quiz. (page 25)

Introduce the vocabulary list for Section 5. (page 8)

LESSON 6

Read Chapters 10-11. Place the vocabulary words in context and discuss their meanings.

Choose a vocabulary activity. (page 9)

Make a mobile by sequencing story events. (page 31)

Plan an incredible journey. Then write a story about it. (page 32)

Write a front page newspaper story about the incredible journey. (page 33)

Write about a wish that came true. (page 34)

Administer the Section 5 quiz. (page 30)

LESSON 7

Assign After the Book activities. (pages 35 and 36)

Begin work on culminating activities. (pages 37, 38, 39, 40 and 41)

LESSON 8

Administer unit tests 1, 2, and/or 3. (pages 42, 43, and 44)

Discuss the test answers and possibilities.

Discuss students' enjoyment of the book.

Provide a list of related reading for your students. (page 45)

Before the Book

Before students begin reading *The Incredible Journey*, use some pre-reading activities to stimulate their interest, improve their comprehension, and involve them in this classic.

1. Have students predict what the story is about just by looking at the title and the cover illustration.

2. Divide the class into cooperative learning groups. Have students work together to do research and write a report about the Ojibway Indians.

3. Read aloud to the class and discuss the quote which is located at the beginning of the book from Walt Whitman's *Leaves of Grass*.

4. Have students predict story events by previewing the illustrations in the book.

5. Answer the following questions:

    • Are you interested in

    . . . stories about animals?

    . . . stories about loyalty?

    . . . stories that tell about an adventure?

    . . . stories that involve danger and suspense?

    • Would you ever

    . . . make a decision based on your feelings instead of hard facts?

    . . . take a risk for a cause you believe in and ask others to do the same?

    . . . risk others' lives to get what you want?

6. Have students choose a topic about which they feel strongly. Ask them to write a story that will persuade others to believe as they do.

7. Teach a lesson about similes by showing how to use "like" or "as" to compare two or more things.

8. Have students work with a partner to do research about Labrador retrievers, English bull terriers, and Siamese cats. Ask students to draw a picture and write a description of each animal.

About the Author

Sheila Burnford was born on May 11, 1918, in Scotland. She was the daughter of Wilfred George Cochrane and Ida Phillip (Macmillan) Every. She was educated in Scotland, England, and Germany. In 1941, she married Dr. David Burnford. Within several years, Sheila and her husband had three children.

Sheila Burnford is a self-employed writer. She has written articles for newspapers and magazines. In 1964, some of her articles were published in a book entitled *Fields of Noon*. She has also written novels such as *The Incredible Journey*, *Without Reserve*, *One Woman's Arctic*, and *Mr. Noah and the Second Flood*. *The Incredible Journey*, which was published in 1961, has won many awards.

The English bull terrier, Siamese cat, and Labrador retriever that are described in *The Incredible Journey* are based on pets that Sheila Burnford and her family had. The family's bull terrier, named Bill, provided Sheila Burnford with comfort and security while she lived in England during World War II. Since her husband was in the Royal Navy and her two oldest children were just babies, she passed the time by reading and talking to Bill.

After the war, Sheila Burnford and her family, including Bill, moved to Canada. Bill was lonely when the children were at school all day, so the family acquired Simon, a Siamese kitten, to be a companion for Bill. The dog and cat developed an extremely close relationship. They slept in the same basket and hunted and played together. Eventually, Sheila Burnford's husband got a Labrador retriever. The Labrador was a serious hunting dog, and he would never play or hunt with Bill and Simon. However, as Bill got older and began to lose his eyesight, the young Labrador became his understanding and patient guardian. The Labrador would accompany Bill as he made his daily rounds to investigate the fire hydrants and garbage cans in the neighborhood. They would always arrive home safely because the Labrador would guide Bill back to the sidewalk whenever he strayed onto the road.

The heartwarming story told in *The Incredible Journey* continues to be very popular. Over the years, it has been translated into many different languages and was made into a movie by Walt Disney. The movie version of this story has been remade, using the title *Homeward Bound*.

6

The Incredible Journey
By Sheila Burnford
Bantam-Skylark, 1987

(Available in Canada, Doubleday Dell Seal; UK, Chivers Pub.; AUS, Transworld Pub.)

This story is about three pets that begin a journey in the northwestern part of Ontario, a Canadian province. The area is described as "Thousands of miles of country roads, rough timber lanes, overgrown tracks leading to abandoned mines, and unmapped trails snake across its length and breadth." There are trappers, hunters, Indians, pioneers and others who want to enjoy the land and the freedom it offers. "But all these human beings together are as a handful of sand upon the great ocean shores, and for the most part there is silence and solitude and an uninterrupted way of life for the wild animals that abound there. . . ."

The trio is made up of a Siamese cat, an English bull terrier, and a Labrador retriever. Tao, the slender Siamese cat, is wheat colored with "chocolate colored front paws curved in towards one another" and has sapphire eyes. The old white English bull terrier, Bodger, has "a deep-chested stocky body and a whip-tapered tail." His brown eyes, which are "sunk deep within pinkish rims," are slanted and almond shaped. His ears are large and rectangular. Although Bodger was bred to fight and endure, he is a docile and devoted family pet. Luath is the large red gold Labrador retriever. He is a young dog with a "powerful build, broad noble head, and a deep, blunt, gentle mouth."

Tao, Bodger, and Luath are staying with John Longridge for a few months while their beloved masters, the Hunters, are away in England. Just three weeks before the Hunters get back, John goes on vacation, asking his housekeeper to care for the trio. The animals do not realize how soon their masters will be returning for them. As a result, Luath decides he must travel home if he wants to be reunited with his masters. Bodger and Tao decide to follow him.

The story describes what happens to Tao, Bodger, and Luath as they travel 250 miles across the Canadian wilderness. Their adventure leads them to encounters with porcupines, a lynx, and a bear and her cub. Day after day they struggle to make this "incredible journey." It is their unconditional love for the Hunters and sheer determination which allows these three pets to overcome even the most difficult obstacles.

Vocabulary Lists

SECTION 1
(Chapters 1-2)

sprawling	amphibious
austerely	irrepressible
sybaritic	assented
reciprocal	province
contrition	barbarian
mellow	adjacent
pursuit	placid
gait	wary
contented	acute
obedient	instinct

SECTION 2
(Chapters 3-4)

staggered	ravenous
sedge	abhorrent
remote	adversary
undaunted	transformation
sauntered	aloof
forage	ambling
cantering	grimace
paroxysms	mirth
hospitality	derision
guttural	reluctant

SECTION 3
(Chapters 5-6)

trio	disposition
lodestone	clamorous
complacent	marauding
bracken	fastidiously
submerged	affectionately
frugal	bedraggled
heraldic	incongruous
undeterred	austerity
interval	condescension
quiver	impulsively

SECTION 4
(Chapters 7-9)

apparition	capitulate
voraciously	cunning
poseur	insolence
jaunty	delectable
pliant	abandoned
grotesquely	detested
obscurity	mutinous
ingratiating	impetus
recumbent	infuriated
baffled	desolate

SECTION 5
(Chapters 10-11)

panorama	catastrophe	qualms
disparate	intolerant	poignant
incredulous	inconsolable	inarticulate
gallivanting	surly	precarious
despondent	coincidental	acute
diffidently	conjured	indistinguishable
wryly	penitent	

8

Vocabulary Activity Ideas

To prepare your students to learn and retain the necessary vocabulary for *The Incredible Journey,* here are some fun and interesting activities to try.

Prepare a spinner to play **Spin-A-Word** by drawing lines to divide the spinner into four equal parts. Mark each part with one of the following point values: 10 points, 20 points, 30 points, 40 points. Divide the class into two teams. Play the game by having each student spin the spinner and define a vocabulary word that you provide. A correct answer is worth the point value shown on the spinner. Then the spinner goes to the other team. A wrong answer means the spinner goes to the other team without any points being scored. The team with the highest total score is the winner at the end of a period of time that you designate.

Have students create a **Wordsearch** or a **Crossword Puzzle** to exchange with a partner. Then have them check each other's paper.

Ask your students to **Write a Story** using the vocabulary words. Point out that students should use the vocabulary words in such a way that they have the same meaning as expressed in the story. Have students read their story to the class. Then display the stories in the hallway for other students to enjoy.

Have students record the vocabulary words and their definitions in a **Vocabulary Journal** that they can keep when they are finished reading the book. You may wish to laminate the cover of their journals so they will last longer.

Challenge your students to a **Vocabulary Bee**. The rules to this are very similar to a Spelling Bee, except that students must define the word as well as correctly spell it.

Divide the class into cooperative learning groups. Then have students work together to create an **Illustrated Dictionary** for the vocabulary words.

Before students enter the classroom, hide index cards around the room, some with vocabulary words written on them and others with definitions on them. When the class arrives, divide them into two teams to play **Vocabulary Hide and Seek**. Allow students to search the room for a period of time that you designate. Teams can score a point by matching a word with its definition. The winning team is the one with the most points at the end of the time period.

Quiz

1. On the back of this paper, write a one-paragraph summary of this section. When writing your summary, be sure to use a topic sentence that tells the main idea. Then, give supporting details that describe the major events of each chapter.

2. Why are the English bull terrier, Siamese cat, and Labrador retriever staying with John Longridge?

    _____

    _____

3. What decision did the Labrador make that affects himself as well as the other two pets, John Longridge, and the Hunter family?

    _____

    _____

4. What does the author mean when she writes, "But all these human beings together are as a handful of sand upon the great ocean shores, . . . "?

    _____

    _____

5. What three events give hints that the animals may not be at the house when John Longridge returns from his trip?

    _____

    _____

6. Why didn't John worry about the animals being alone outside when he left for his vacation?

    _____

    _____

7. Why did Mrs. Oakes assume that John had taken the animals with him?

    _____

    _____

8. How do we know that the animals are no longer in their home environment?

    _____

    _____

9. In what direction did the Labrador think his "beloved master's home" was?

    _____

    _____

10. What was "clear and certain" to the Labrador?

    _____

    _____

Map Making

The Incredible Journey takes place in Canada. Canada is a very large country with vast wilderness areas. Most of the people reside along the southern border. Few people live in the interior part of Canada because of three natural barriers. These barriers are the frozen Arctic region which lies to the north, the Rocky Mountains which are located in the west, and the Canadian Shield which runs along Hudson Bay. The southern part of the Canadian Shield is an area of thick forests growing in thin soil. The northern part of the Shield turns into tundra with soil that is muddy on top and frozen underneath.

Locate a map of Canada in an atlas, encyclopedia, or other reference book. Then on the map below, locate and label the places and geographic features listed in the box. After you have finished labeling your map, you may wish to color it.

British Columbia	**Alberta**	**Saskatchewan**	**Manitoba**
Ontario	**Quebec**	**Nova Scotia**	**New Brunswick**
Newfoundland	**Yukon Territory**	**Northwest Territories**	**Pacific Ocean**
Hudson Bay	**Lake Superior**	**Lake Huron**	**Lake Michigan**
Lake Erie	**Lake Ontario**	**Rocky Mountains**	**Atlantic Ocean**
Labrador Sea	**Baffin Bay**	**Ottawa**	

KEY:
— · · — International Border
— · — Provincial Border
✪ National Capital

Industry

Sheila Burnford helps us get a better mental image of the story's setting by describing some of the occupations of the people who live there. She writes, "It is a country of far flung, lonely farms and a few widely scattered small towns and villages, of lonely trappers' shacks and logging camps. Most of its industry comes from the great pulp and paper companies who work their timber concessions deep in the very heart of the forests; and from the mines, for it is rich in minerals."

Think about the area in which you live. What type of occupations do people have? How do the natural resources of your area influence the types of occupations people have? For example, if you live in Oregon, you will notice that many people work in timber-related industries because of the abundance of trees.

Use the chart below to tell about some of the occupations of people in your area. In addition to using your own knowledge, you may wish to use community resources such as the Chamber of Commerce, reference books, such as encyclopedias and almanacs, and information obtained by interviewing friends and family members. After you have completed the chart, write a paragraph on the back of this page to compare and contrast the occupations in your area with those in the part of Canada where the story takes place.

OCCUPATIONS	INFLUENCES

Glaciers

The terrain where *The Incredible Journey* takes place is described as "a deeply wooded wilderness — of endless chains of lonely lakes and rushing rivers." These rivers and lakes were formed by glaciers several hundreds of years ago. *Glaciers* are described as huge masses of ice that slowly flow over the land. They are formed in the cold Arctic regions or on very high mountains. The extremely low temperatures in these areas enable the large amounts of snow to build up and turn to ice.

Glaciers change the land in many ways. As they move under the pressure of their own weight, glaciers pick up debris, such as rocks, dirt, and gravel. They often break rocks, leave huge cracks called crevasses, round the tops of ridges and mountain peaks, deposit debris into drifts, polish or scratch bedrock, and dig out valleys. They may increase or decrease in size as the climate changes over very long periods of time. Some of the snow and ice from glaciers will melt and become water. Water from a melting glacier is called meltwater. Meltwater creates streams and rivers which flow to the ocean. Sometimes meltwater also forms lakes.

Some major glaciers cover regions in the northwestern part of North America. The most famous one is the 840-square-mile Malaspina Glacier of Yakutat Bay in Alaska. Other glaciers include those in Banff National Park in Alberta, Glacier National Park in Montana, and Mount Rainier National Park in Washington.

Work together with three or four other students to do research about glaciers. Ask yourself the following questions as you do your research: What are the different kinds of glaciers called? What are the characteristics of the different types of glaciers? Where can glaciers still be found? What are some interesting facts about existing glaciers? Then make a travel brochure that explains what glaciers are and describes some glaciers that would be interesting to visit. You may wish to include a diagram of a glacier in your brochure.

Situations Beyond Your Control

Sometimes we do not have control over the situations in which we find ourselves. When this happens, it can be very frustrating and upsetting. This is what has happened to the Hunters' three pets. When Jim Hunter got a teaching job in England, he asked John Longridge to watch after the family's three pets for the next several months until their return from England. John takes good care of the three animals and comes to love them as if they were his own. However, when John leaves on his vacation, the animals do not understand why he has left. They miss the Hunter family very much. As a result, the Labrador retriever decides that if he wants to see the Hunters ever again, he must go to their home which is 250 miles away. This is how the three pets begin their incredible journey.

Think about times when you have felt like you were in a situation over which you had no control. These experiences might include the death of a family member, the death of a pet, having to move, or having to start at a new school. When we have no control over a situation we are in, we often feel helpless to try to make our situation better.

Think about a situation over which you felt like you had no control. Write a paragraph to describe the situation and explain how you dealt with it.

Use this page to organize your thoughts before beginning your paragraph.

- **Situation:** _____

_____

_____

_____

- **My feelings:** _____

_____

_____

_____

- **Why I had no control:** _____

_____

_____

_____

_____

Quiz

1. On the back of this paper, write a one-paragraph summary of this section. When writing your summary, be sure to use a topic sentence that tells the main idea. Then give supporting details that describe the major events of each chapter.

2. What considerations did the Labrador make for the bull terrier while they were traveling?

    _____

    _____

3. Why was killing an animal for food abhorrent to the Labrador?

    _____

    _____

4. What happened that enraged the bear, and how did the bull terrier escape?

    _____

    _____

5. How did the cat and the Labrador help keep the bull terrier alive in this section?

    _____

    _____

6. How long did it take the old dog to recover enough so he could start traveling again?

    _____

    _____

7. How did the Ojibways help the cat and the bull terrier?

    _____

    _____

8. Why didn't the Labrador visit the Ojibways?

    _____

    _____

9. What did the Ojibways consider the bull terrier to be?

    _____

    _____

10. Why did the Ojibways believe that the omen would prove fortunate?

    _____

    _____

Collecting Data and Graphing

In chapters 3 and 4, Luath, Bodger, and Tao are very hungry as they make their journey across the Canadian wilderness. They are not used to hunting for every morsel of food. As a result, every source of food is extremely important to their survival. Reread the two chapters, and collect data on how many and what kind of wild animals the dogs and cat are able to hunt and kill for food. On the graph shown at the top, draw bars to represent the number of wild animals eaten by each dog and the cat. On the graph shown at the bottom, draw bars to represent the kinds of wild animals eaten. If you are not sure which animals belong in each category, look for the information in a reference book such as a dictionary or encyclopedia.

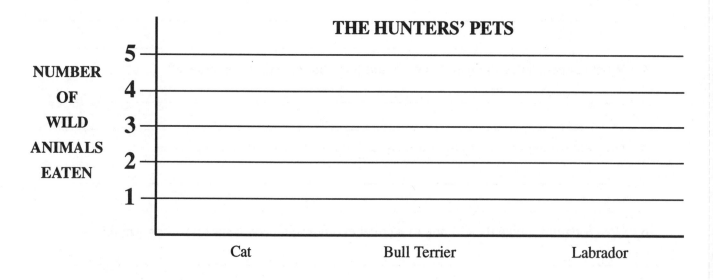

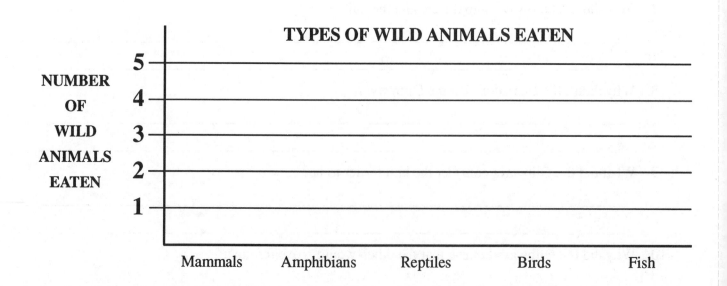

A Multicultural View

The three animals are attracted to an Ojibway Indian camp by the smell of food cooking over an open fire. The bull terrier is the first to enter the camp. The Indians feed him chunks of meat as he begs for more. Then the Siamese cat comes into the camp and takes a piece of meat away from the bull terrier, without a single protest from the dog. As a result the Indians think that the Spirits have sent the bull terrier to test their hospitality. Since the Indians have treated the dog well, they believe that this is an omen of good fortune.

The Ojibways' belief in omens is an important part of their culture. They believe that an omen of good fortune will allow them to be more successful at fishing, hunting, and gathering wild plants. The Ojibways feel that fortunate omens will ensure that the birch bark remains plentiful, so they can continue to use it for making canoes, boxes, dishes, and baskets, and for covering their shelters, called wigwams.

Today, most of the Ojibways live in Michigan, Minnesota, and Wisconsin, in the United States, as well as the Canadian province of Ontario. They harvest most of the wild rice that is eaten in the United States.

With a partner, do research to investigate the Indian tribes who have lived or are living in your area. Remember to look for information that tells you about their way of life, system of beliefs, food, homes, clothing, and celebrations. You may use reference materials; personal interviews; periodicals, such as newspapers and magazines; community resources, such as the Chamber of Commerce; or other sources that you find helpful.

Write a short report based on your research. Make an illustration to go with your report. Then, share your report and illustration by giving an oral presentation to the class.

Imagery

Imagery is the use of words that appeal to any of the five senses: seeing, hearing, feeling, smelling, and tasting. Authors often use imagery to create mental pictures for the reader. For example, Sheila Burnford uses imagery when she describes what attracts the two dogs and the cat to the Ojibway Indian camp. She states, "The scent on the evening breeze was a fragrant compound of roasting rice, wild-duck stew and wood smoke." It is almost possible for you to smell these odors because of the words Sheila Burnford has chosen.

Skim chapters 3 and 4 to find examples of imagery for each of the events listed below. Quote the sentences which helped you have a mental image of these events. Then, use the boxes below to draw a picture of your mental images.

1.   the bull terrier struggling to keep up with the Labrador and the cat

_____

_____

2.   the cat jumping on the bear cub's back

_____

_____

3.   the Labrador waiting for the bull terrier and the cat to return from the Ojibway camp

_____

_____

①	②	③

Taking Responsibility for a Pet

When the bull terrier and the cat show up at the Ojibway camp, they receive a very warm welcome. The Indians feed the two animals and give them a warm place to sleep. In addition, they treat the dog and cat with kindness. They would have gladly given the bull terrier and the cat a home if they had wanted to stay. However, the Labrador summons the bull terrier and the cat so they can return to their real home with the family they have always loved.

Pretend that you have found a stray dog or cat. Your family has asked many people in the neighborhood if anyone owns this animal, but no one claims it. This stray does not have a home to go to like the two dogs and the cat in *The Incredible Journey.* You have asked your parents for permission to keep this animal. They agree to let you keep the animal if you will care for it.

In the box below, make a list of the things you would have to do to be a responsible pet owner. Then write a paragraph persuading other pet owners to take good care of their pets.

The following are ways to properly care for a pet.

1. _____

2. _____

3. _____

4. _____

5. _____

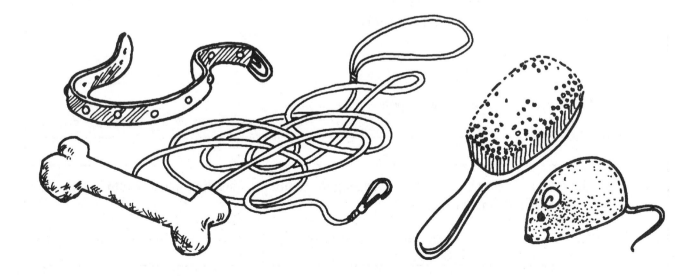

Quiz

1. On the back of this paper, write a one-paragraph summary of this section. When writing your summary be sure to use a topic sentence that tells the main idea. Then give supporting details that describe the major events of each chapter.

2. Why is the Labrador really suffering in comparison to the other two animals?

   _____

   _____

3. Describe the old man's unusual treatment of the animals.

   _____

   _____

4. How far is the cat swept downstream?

   _____

   _____

5. Describe Helvi and her family.

   _____

   _____

6. How does Reino Nurmi figure out the cat is deaf?

   _____

   _____

7. Describe the legend which explains why a Siamese cat has a crooked tail.

   _____

   _____

8. How long does the cat stay with the Nurmis?

   _____

   _____

9. Why does Helvi cry when the cat responds to her voice?

   _____

   _____

10. When the cat leaves Helvi, he is described using the simile ". . . stealing like a wraith in the night . . . ." What does this mean?

   _____

   _____

A Beaver Dam

In this section, the trio arrive at the banks of a river and must swim to get to the other side. The cat is especially hesitant about jumping into the water because he is afraid. Yet, he has no idea just how dangerous crossing that river will be. Two miles upstream there is a beaver dam in a small creek that was built many years ago. After the beavers left, the dam began crumbling and falling apart a little bit at a time. As the cat finally musters enough courage to jump into the river and swim across it, the beaver dam breaks, sweeping the cat downstream.

Examine the diagram of a beaver's lodge and dam that is shown below. Then, use the diagram to construct a model of a beaver's lodge and dam. You may wish to use a variety of materials such as cardboard, construction paper, clay, twigs, fabric, and straws for building your model.

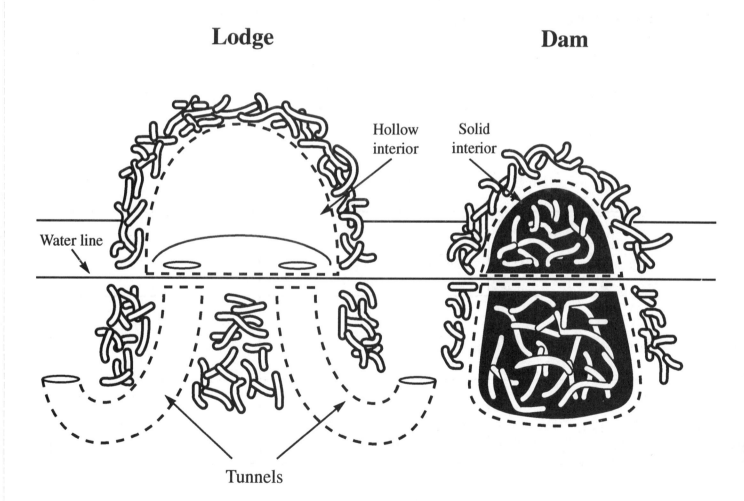

Identifying Character Traits

An author often gives us clues about a character's traits through the descriptions and actions of the character. For example, reread how Sheila Burnford describes the old man that the three animals meet in this section.

"The old man did not pause: small and bent, he hobbled quickly past, lifting an ancient green felt hat from the crown of white hair as he went, and nodding to the dog with a brief smile of great sweetness . . . . Here the old man set his bag down, knocked on the green door, paused, then opened it, standing courteously aside to motion his following in before him."

The character traits of the old man can include: well-mannered, kind, busy, friendly, hospitable, caring for others.

Work with three or four other students to find examples in the story of a character's description and actions that help you know more about that character's traits. Use the chart below to tell about five characters and their traits.

Character's Name	Information from the Story About that Character	Character's Traits

Predicting Outcomes

The three animals have no idea whether they will survive their journey. Each animal has had to struggle to make it this far. For example, Tao, the cat, is deathly afraid of crossing the river. Finally, he decides he will swim to the other side so he can be with his friends. As he proceeds to jump into the river, a beaver dam that is located upstream gives way. The cat is washed downstream. The two dogs try to save the cat, but their effort is in vain. The cat almost drowns and ends up quite a few miles downstream. Fortunately, he is rescued by a ten-year-old girl named Helvi Nurmi.

Pretend that you are the author of *The Incredible Journey*, and you have decided to write a different outcome for when the three animals reach the river. Use the space below to describe what will happen to the trio.

_____

_____

_____

_____

_____

_____

_____

_____

Adding a New Chapter

The three animals have been traveling for some time. Pretend that you have found them. Use the space below to begin writing a new chapter for the book that tells about your experiences with the trio. Be sure to describe how you find the animals, what condition they are in, what you do to care for them, and whether they stay with you or continue their journey.

Quiz

1. On the back of this paper, write a one-paragraph summary of this section. When writing your summary, be sure to use a topic sentence that tells the main idea. Then give supporting details that describe the major events of each chapter.

2. Why did the old dog capitulate when Tao was a kitten?

   _____

   _____

3. What two major problems do the two dogs encounter as they travel alone, and how do they overcome these problems?

   _____

   _____

4. Give examples of how the cat ensures that he doesn't leave a trace of where he has been.

   _____

   _____

5. How does the cat survive the dangerous encounter he has while traveling alone?

   _____

   _____

6. Describe the reunion of the trio.

   _____

   _____

7. How many miles have the three traveled so far?

   _____

   _____

8. How do the animals meet the Mackenzies?

   _____

   _____

9. How do the Mackenzies help the animals?

   _____

   _____

10. Why will the last 50 miles be the toughest part of the trip?

   _____

   _____

Porcupines

As the two dogs continue their journey, they encounter two porcupines. The first porcupine they find is dead. It provides a delicious meal for the dogs. The second porcupine is very much alive. This porcupine and the Labrador have a skirmish, during which the Labrador ends up with quills in his face.

Work with a partner to research porcupines. Fill in the information chart shown below. Then, make a model of a porcupine using clay and toothpicks that you have broken into halves.

Porcupine Information Chart

Description (What does it look like? How big is it? How long does it live?)	
Habitat (Where does it live?)	
Food (What does it eat?)	
Behavior (How does it act?)	
Reproduction (How long does it take for the young to be born? How many young are born? Does it lay eggs or give birth to live young? Where are the young born? Who takes care of the young?)	
Predators (Are there any animals that could kill it?)	
Other (Is there any other interesting information?)	
Sources of Information (Which books were used to gather this information? Note the title of the books, the authors, the publishers, the copyright dates, and the page or pages where the information was found.)	

Canadian Wildlife

During the animals' incredible journey, they encounter many wild animals. Canada has a large variety of wildlife. Use the grid below to make a word search using the names of some of Canada's wildlife that are listed in the box. To make a word search, first fill in the names of the animals by placing one letter in each box. The animal names can be written horizontally, vertically, or diagonally on the grid. Then, fill in the blank spaces with any letters you choose. When you are finished filling in all of the spaces, trade with a classmate and solve each other's word search.

black bear	lynx	porcupine	beaver
moose	muskrat	fox	mink
timber wolf	otter	polar bear	musk oxen
great snowy owl	ptarmigan	gull	Arctic tern
Canada goose	chipmunk	mallard	rainbow trout
perch	rabbit	weasel	raccoon
marten	white-tailed deer	squirrel	whiskyjack

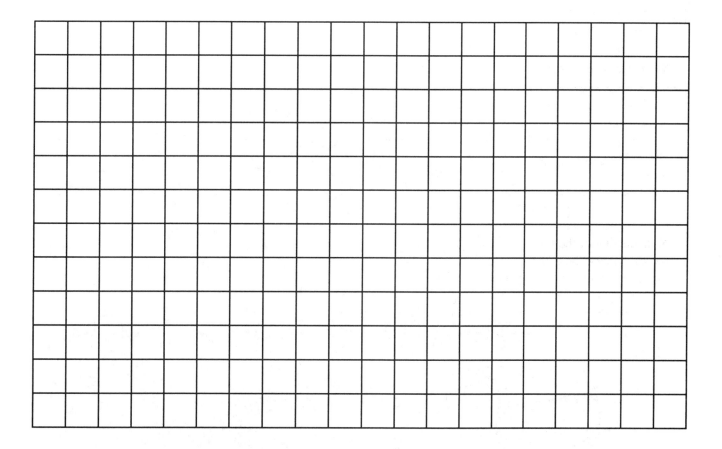

Metric Map Activity

The three animals must travel 250 miles across the Canadian wilderness to reach their home with the Hunters. In Canada, people use the metric system of measurement. The distance between two places is measured in kilometers (km) rather than miles.

Pretend that you are taking a trip to see five cities in Canada. Use the chart below to make a log of the cities you will visit while on your trip. Measure the distance between cities by following these steps: 1) Put the edge of a sheet of paper on the map so that it touches the symbol for the first city. 2) Draw a mark on the paper directly under the symbol for the second city. 3) Place the edge of the paper at 0 on the distance scale on the map. 4) Read the numbers on the scale to measure the distance to the second city's mark. 5) If the distance is longer than the scale, determine how many times the scale will fit between the edge of the paper and the mark. Multiply that number times the highest number on the scale and add any additional kilometers. When you are finished with the chart, draw a line on the map to show where you will go on your trip.

City of Departure	Destination	Distance in Kilometers

KEY:
- — . . — International Border
- — . — Provincial Border
- ✪ National Capitol

SCALE OF KILOMETERS

0   250   500   750   1000

Environmental Connection

"The cat by himself was a swift and efficient traveler . . . . He left no trace of his progress; . . . never a twig cracked, and not a stone was dislodged from under his sure, soft feet." The cat traveled like this so other animals would not know where he was, but this was also beneficial to the environment.

Many people enjoy visiting wilderness areas such as the one the cat found himself traveling across. However, these areas are not always left the way in which they were found. People sometimes take things from the environment, such as flowers or wildlife, and they often leave things, such as trash. Today, most people realize the value of our wilderness areas and are working to preserve them.

With a partner, list some ways that you can help to protect wilderness areas. Then, use a reference book such as a phone book, to identify an organization that helps protect and preserve wilderness areas. Write a letter asking the organization for information about what you can do to make a difference.

1. _____

2. _____

3. _____

4. _____

5. _____

6. _____

7. _____

8. _____

9. _____

10. _____

Quiz

1. On the back of this paper, write a one paragraph summary of this section. When writing your summary, be sure to use a topic sentence that tells the main idea. Then, give supporting details that describe the major events of each chapter.

2. Explain the simile " . . . his thoughts as bleak as the empty, unresponsive house to which he had returned only a short while ago."

   _____

   _____

3. What clues help John piece together what has happened to the animals?

   _____

   _____

4. Why is Mrs. Oakes inconsolable?

   _____

   _____

5. Why does John say, " 'Tonight,...I'd give him the whole bed! I'd even sleep in the basket myself if only he would come back' "?

   _____

   _____

6. What opinions do Peter and Elizabeth have about the fate of each animal?

   _____

   _____

7. List two different reasons why John goes to visit the Hunters.

   _____

   _____

8. What does Peter remember about last year's experience with trying to teach Bodger to be a hunting dog?

   _____

   _____

9. Explain the statement, "And as he had never run before, as though he would outdistance time, Peter was running towards his dog."

   _____

   _____

10. What is the significance of Tao returning for Bodger at the end of the book?

   _____

   _____

Make a Story Mobile

Read and cut out the story events shown below. Glue each event onto a piece of construction paper, and draw a picture on the back. Make a mobile, hanging story events (in order) from a coat hanger with string or yarn. Then ask your teacher to display your mobile.

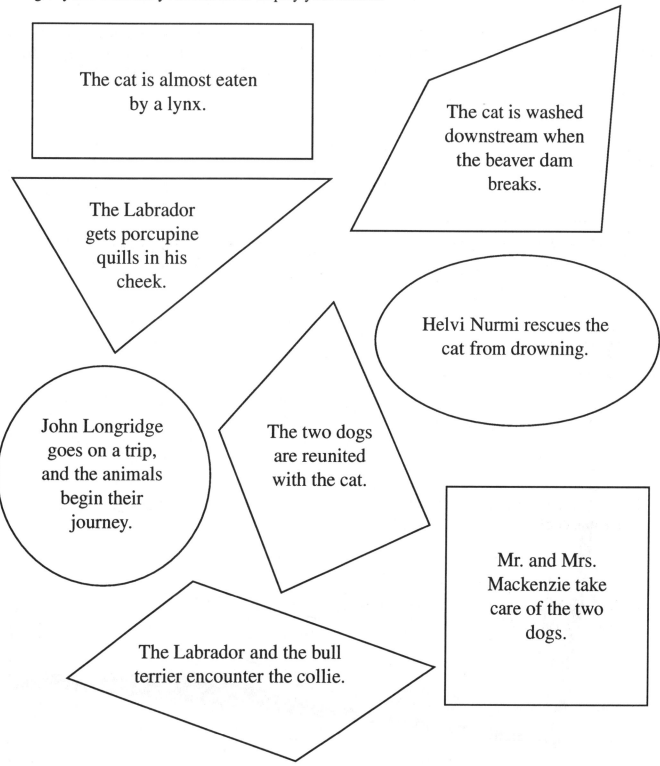

The cat is almost eaten by a lynx.

The cat is washed downstream when the beaver dam breaks.

The Labrador gets porcupine quills in his cheek.

Helvi Nurmi rescues the cat from drowning.

John Longridge goes on a trip, and the animals begin their journey.

The two dogs are reunited with the cat.

Mr. and Mrs. Mackenzie take care of the two dogs.

The Labrador and the bull terrier encounter the collie.

Making an Incredible Journey

By the end of the story, the two dogs and the cat have had several dangerous encounters with other animals. Initially, they had to fight with a bear cub and its mother. Then, when the two dogs were by themselves, they had to survive an encounter with a live porcupine and fend off an attack from a farmer's collie. When the cat was by himself, he narrowly escaped being eaten by a lynx.

Pretend that you have decided to walk the 250 miles that the animals covered on their journey in order to see what it was like. Think about what you would do if you had to make this trip across the Canadian wilderness. Then, write a series of journal entries describing your incredible journey.

In your journal, tell about the following:

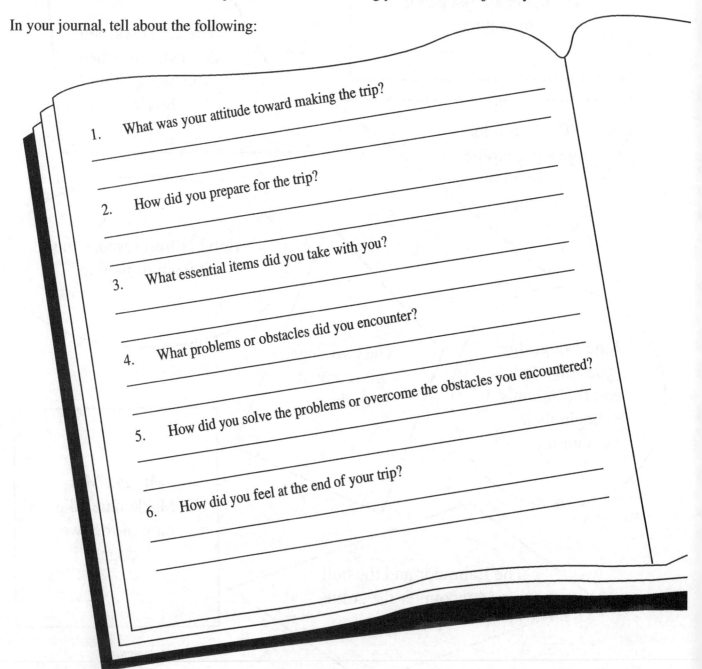

1. What was your attitude toward making the trip?

2. How did you prepare for the trip?

3. What essential items did you take with you?

4. What problems or obstacles did you encounter?

5. How did you solve the problems or overcome the obstacles you encountered?

6. How did you feel at the end of your trip?

EXTRA!! EXTRA!! READ ALL ABOUT IT!!

Pretend that you are a newspaper reporter and you have heard about the incredible journey made by the two dogs and the cat. You have decided to write a front page article about these three amazing animals. Use the space below to write your article. Be sure to answer the questions: who, what, when, where, how, and why. You may wish to include quotes from the characters in the book so it appears you have interviewed some of the people who had contact with the animals while they were traveling.

CANADA NEWS

Wishes Can Come True

Peter Hunter is turning twelve years old. For his birthday, Peter's family and John Longridge take him to the cottage near Lake Windigo. Although everyone is having a good time, they are all thinking about their three missing pets. As the Hunter family and John Longridge are getting ready to leave, Tao and Luath come home. Only Bodger, Peter's pet, has not returned. Peter tries not to show it, but he is very disappointed. Just as Peter is about to give up hope, he sights Bodger running toward him. Peter and Bodger run as quickly as they can to meet each other. They are so enthusiastic about seeing one another, they are unaware of anyone else around them.

Think of a birthday or other type of wish that you have made. You may have felt totally hopeless just as Peter did. However, something happened and your wish came true, just like Peter's wish to have Bodger back home came true. In a paragraph, describe the wish you made and explain what happened.

_____

_____

_____

_____

_____

_____

_____

_____

_____

_____

_____

Writing and Art

Writing Activities

1. Arrange any one of these words vertically in a column: Luath, Bodger, Tao, Incredible, Journey. Write a poem related to the story in which the first word of each line begins with a letter in the column.

2. Work with three or four other students to add a new scene to the book. In this new scene, describe an experience the trio has with an animal they have not already encountered in the story. Then, role-play the scene you have created.

3. Pretend that the animals have shown up at your house just as they did at the Nurmis' and the Mackenzies'. Write a paragraph describing the condition the animals are in and how you cared for them.

4. Imagine that you have been asked to interview Sheila Burnford. What are some questions you might ask her? With a partner, make list of questions you would ask. Then, answer those questions the way you predict Sheila Burnford would.

5. Maple sugar was first produced by the Indians of Canada long before European explorers came to North America. Write a paragraph describing how you think the Indians discovered the "sweet water" and how they learned to make maple products by heating the maple sugar.

Art Activities

1. Choose your favorite part of the story. Then create a display for this part of the story by drawing, painting, building a diorama, or using clay.

2. Work with two or three other students to create a poster or a mural of the beautiful wilderness area the trio travel across. Display your posters or murals on the walls in the classroom or the school library.

3. Long ago, the Indians of Canada began carving totem poles to represent their family, clan, or tribal pride and prosperity. Pretend you are an Ojibway Indian. Construct a totem pole to represent your tribe's ideals.

Let's Go to the Movies!

The story from *The Incredible Journey* has been remade into a new movie entitled *Homeward Bound*. As a culminating activity, show the video to your class. Have students look for similarities and differences between the book and the movie. At the conclusion of the movie, have a class discussion.

Use the following ideas to guide the discussion.

  Make a chart to help students compare and contrast the movie and the book.

  Have students tell which they prefer: the book or the movie. Then, have them explain their preference.

Venn Diagram

A *Venn diagram* is a pictorial representation using circles which allows you to compare information. The parts of the circle that do not overlap show what is unique to each subject. The overlapping part of the circles is in the middle and shows what is common to both the movie and the book. Using the Venn diagram, write things from the movie and the book that were unique about each, and in the middle state what the book and the movie have in common.

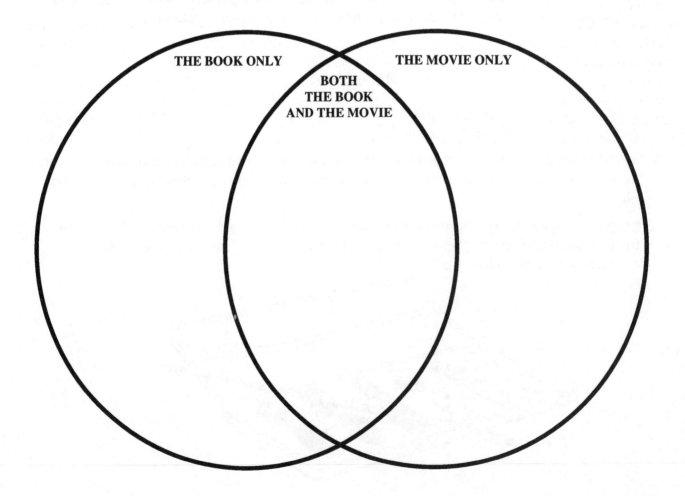

It Takes a Writer

Authors use different writing techniques to give the reader a specific type of experience. As you read *The Incredible Journey*, you learned about some of the ways Sheila Burnford made this story special. She used imagery, or vivid descriptions, which appeal to one or more of the five senses. She gave you hints about a character's traits when she described what that character's appearance and actions were like. She also provided clues that helped readers predict upcoming events in the story.

Now you will have the opportunity to apply some of the skills you learned in this unit. You will write a theme using some of the same techniques that Sheila Burnford used in her story.

Essay

For your topic in this activity, you will be exploring how problem solving is an important theme in *The Incredible Journey*. You will use process-writing skills to break down the task into five steps: outlining, writing a rough draft, editing and revising, making a final draft, sharing your final draft.

Before you begin writing, you will need to skim through the story and take notes about information that is related to your problem-solving topic. You may wish to organize your notes on index cards. Whether you use index cards or pieces of paper, be sure to write down the page numbers where the information is located as you take notes. This will help you return to that information if you need to recheck it for any reason. After your note-taking is complete, you will need to organize your notes using the outline format provided on page 38. Your outline will help you write your rough draft according to the guidelines shown on page 39. Your rough draft will include the following parts: a title, an introductory paragraph, paragraphs that are the body of the report, and a concluding paragraph. Once you have edited and revised your rough draft, you will want to use your best handwriting to make a final draft of your essay. Then, find a way to share your essay with the class.

It Takes a Writer: The Outline

An outline is a special way of organizing information. It begins with a title that describes the general topic of the outline. The information presented in the outline is usually written using phrases with only the first word of each phrase starting with a capital letter. An outline format is organized as follows: Each main topic is marked with a Roman numeral followed by a period. A main topic tells what is in that major section of the outline. A subtopic is marked by a capital letter followed by a period. A subtopic tells the facts and ideas that support the main topics. A detail is marked by an Arabic numeral followed by a period. A detail gives very specific information about a subtopic.

Use the outline format below to tell about a couple of problems the two dogs and the cat encountered and the solutions they came up with for those problems.

Title: Problem Solving in *The Incredible Journey*

I. Understanding problems

    A. _____

        1. _____

        2. _____

    B. _____

        1. _____

        2. _____

II. Finding solutions

    A. _____

        1. _____

        2. _____

    B. _____

        1. _____

        2. _____

It Takes a Writer: The Rough Draft

Using your outline as a guide write your rough draft on the back of this page. After you have finished your rough draft, you will want to put it away for awhile and read it later. Closely examine it for capitalization, punctuation, and grammatical errors. Be sure the essay flows smoothly and makes sense. Edit and revise it as needed. Then read it to a friend, and let that person suggest ways to improve it. Make additional changes based on these suggestions. When you are finished editing and revising, neatly recopy your essay to make a final draft. Find a way to share your story with the class, such as reading it aloud or displaying it on a bulletin board.

Following is an explanation of the parts that go into making a rough draft and a final draft.

Title: Problem Solving in *The Incredible Journey*

Introductory Paragraph: State the reason for your essay. Include information that will grab the reader's attention so he or she will want to read your story.

Body of the Story: Develop your theme. Be sure every paragraph includes a topic sentence that states the main idea. Give at least three details to support each main idea. (You can use the outline for this purpose to help you.) These details can be a description of events from the book using your own words or they can be specific quotes. If you use a quote, remember to use quotation marks and copy the words exactly as they are written. Be sure to include imagery, as well as clues that will help the reader recognize character traits and predict story events.

Concluding Paragraph: This lets the reader know that the essay is ending. You will need to summarize your main ideas.

Use the following format when writing your rough and final drafts:

> **Title**
>
> **Introductory Paragraph**
>
> **Body Paragraphs**
>
> **Concluding Paragraph**

Design a Book Cover

An important element to every piece of literature is the work done by the artist on the illustrations throughout the book. It is very important to grab the reader's eye by having a book cover that captures the imagination. The cover needs to include the book's title, the author's name, and a scene depicting the book. Create a book cover that will make people want to read *The Incredible Journey*.

French Influence

The animals came across several farms while traveling. Towards the end of the story, they finally met the Mackenzies. The couple took good care of the two dogs and gave them food, shelter, and medical attention for a couple of days. The Mackenzies' home life is like that of other farmers in Ontario.

Ontario has thousands of farmers. They produce large quantities of milk, butter, eggs, and poultry. Ontario is also a leading producer of fruits and vegetables.

Many people in Ontario are of French descent. They love to cook and eat specialized French foods. One of these foods is known as crepes. Crepes are thin, flat pancakes that may be eaten plain or with filling. Below are the recipes for crepes, the filling, and a sauce to pour on top. Be sure to work under the direction of an adult and follow kitchen safety rules.

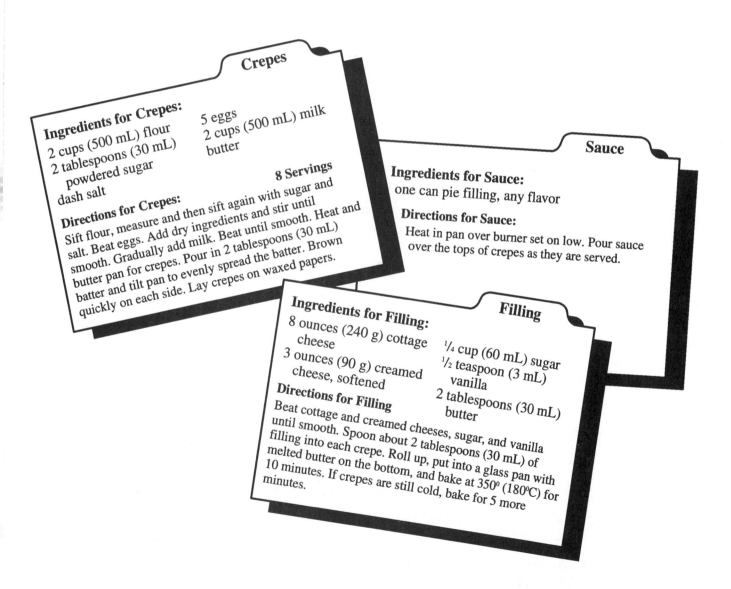

Crepes

Ingredients for Crepes:
2 cups (500 mL) flour
2 tablespoons (30 mL) powdered sugar
dash salt
5 eggs
2 cups (500 mL) milk
butter

8 Servings

Directions for Crepes:
Sift flour, measure and then sift again with sugar and salt. Beat eggs. Add dry ingredients and stir until smooth. Gradually add milk. Beat until smooth. Heat and butter pan for crepes. Pour in 2 tablespoons (30 mL) batter and tilt pan to evenly spread the batter. Brown quickly on each side. Lay crepes on waxed papers.

Sauce

Ingredients for Sauce:
one can pie filling, any flavor

Directions for Sauce:
Heat in pan over burner set on low. Pour sauce over the tops of crepes as they are served.

Filling

Ingredients for Filling:
8 ounces (240 g) cottage cheese
3 ounces (90 g) creamed cheese, softened
¼ cup (60 mL) sugar
½ teaspoon (3 mL) vanilla
2 tablespoons (30 mL) butter

Directions for Filling
Beat cottage and creamed cheeses, sugar, and vanilla until smooth. Spoon about 2 tablespoons (30 mL) of filling into each crepe. Roll up, put into a glass pan with melted butter on the bottom, and bake at 350º (180ºC) for 10 minutes. If crepes are still cold, bake for 5 more minutes.

Unit Test

Matching: Match these quotes with the characters they describe.

Helvi Nurmi	Hunter Family	John Longridge	Ojibways	Mackenzies

1. _____ "The men were a colorful lot in jeans and bright plaid shirts, but the women were dressed in somber colors."

2. _____ ". . . down by the river, skipping flat stones across the water, and wishing that she had a companion."

3. _____ "He was a tall, austerely pleasant man of about forty, . . ."

4. _____ ". . . watching the panorama of the river, . . . returning from their long stay in England."

5. _____ "They were an elderly couple, . . . living alone now in a big farmhouse . . . ."

True or False: Write true or false next to each statement below.

1. _____ The Hunters had asked the trio to come home.
2. _____ John Longridge would have liked to have taken the animals with him on his trip.
3. _____ Helvi Nurmi cried when the cat left because he was her only friend.
4. _____ The cat was bitten by the lynx before he could escape.
5. _____ The three animals never made it back to the Hunters.

Short Answers: Provide a short answer for each question.

1. What is driving Luath, the Labrador retriever, to make this incredible journey? _____

   _____

2. How did the Labrador encourage the bull terrier and the cat to cross the river? _____

   _____

3. Why was the Labrador surprised when the second porcupine fought back? _____

   _____

4. What did John do to find the animals? _____

   _____

5. Why does the cat run to meet Bodger, the bull terrier, at the end of the story? _____

   _____

Essays: Respond to these essay questions on the back of this paper.

1. How could you tell that Luath was obsessed with going home to the Hunters? Justify your answer with examples from the story.

2. What is the meaning of this statement: "Longridge had never thought of himself as being a particularly emotional man, but when the Labrador appeared an instant later, a gaunt, stare-coated shadow of the beautiful dog he had last seen, . . . he felt a lump in his throat,. . ."?

Responses

Explain the meaning of each of these quotations from *The Incredible Journey*.

Chapter 1: *"When the pale fingers of the moon reached over the young dog in the back kitchen he stirred in his uneasy sleep, then sat upright, his ears pricked—listening and listening for the sound that never came: the high, piercing whistle of his master . . . ."*

Chapter 2: *"Presently all three disappeared from sight down the dusty road, trotting briskly and with purpose."*

Chapter 3: *"The old dog lay unconscious and remote."*

Chapter 4: *"All this time the young dog crouched on the hillside, motionless and watchful, although every driving, urgent nerve in his body fretted and strained at the delay."*

Chapter 5: *"Alone now, with a brief moment of freedom from the constant daytime urging, the old dog made the most of it."*

Chapter 6: *"But on the fourth night he was restless, shaking his head and pawing his ears, his voice distressed at her back."*

Chapter 7: *"The dog, for the first time and last time in his life, capitulated."*

Chapter 8: *"Age-old instinct told him to leave no trace of his passing; . . ."*

Chapter 9: *"Most of the way now lay through the Strellon Game Reserve, country that was more desolate and rugged than anything they had yet encountered."*

Chapter 10: *"Again the half-submerged memory distracted him: Luath's eyes . . . some difference in the pattern of his behavior . . . Luath's behavior on the last morning, the gesture of his unexpected paw . . . With a sudden flash of insight, he understood at last."*

Chapter 11: *"It was Tao, returning for his old friend, that they might end their journey together."*

Conversations

Work in size-appropriate groups to write and perform the conversations that might have occurred in each of the following situations.

- John Longridge talks to the animals as he is leaving for his trip. *(4 people)*

- Mr. and Mrs. Oakes get the house ready for John's departure. *(2 people)*

- The animals discuss what to do after John has left on his vacation. *(3 people)*

- The cat explains why he is hesitant to follow the dogs at the beginning of the journey. *(3 people)*

- The three animals encounter the bear and her cub. *(5 people)*

- The Ojibways are entertained by the bull terrier. *(8 people)*

- The Ojibways discuss how to care for the bull terrier and the cat. *(8 people)*

- The trio meet the old man who wears a green felt hat. *(4 people)*

- The cat expresses his fears about crossing the river. *(3 people)*

- Helvi Nurmi and her parents rescue the cat. *(4 people)*

- Helvi Nurmi tells her parents what she has learned about Siamese cats. *(3 people)*

- The farmer and the collie chase after the Labrador and bull terrier for stealing a chicken. *(4 people)*

- The dogs and cat are reunited and tell about the adventures they had while separated. *(3 people)*

- The Mackenzies discuss what to do about the two dogs they have found. *(2 people)*

- John Longridge and Mrs. Oakes figure out where the three animals have gone. *(2 people)*

- John Longridge tries to console Mrs. Oakes. *(2 people)*

- The Hunters excitedly discuss what they will do after arriving back in Canada. *(4 people)*

- John Longridge and the Hunter family go camping to celebrate Peter's twelfth birthday. *(5 people)*

- Elizabeth is reunited with Tao while she is taking a walk with her family and John Longridge. *(5 people)*

- The Hunter family and John Longridge discuss how incredible it is that the cat and the Labrador have survived their 250 mile journey. *(5 people)*

- John Longridge returns to the cottage to tell the Hunter family that Peter has been reunited with Bodger, the old bull terrier. *(4 people)*

Bibliography

Fiction

Adams, Richard. *Watership Down.* (Avon, 1976)

Branscum, Robbie. *Murder of Hound Dog Bates.* (Viking Penguin, 1982)

Brenner, Barbara. *Mystery of the Disappearing Dogs.* (Alfred A. Knopf, 1982)

DeJong, Meindert. *Shadrach.* (Harper and Row Junior Books, 1980)

Eckert, Allan. *Incident at Hawk's Hill.* (Bantam, 1987)

Fox, Paula. *One-Eyed Cat.* (Bradbury Press, 1984)

Gardiner, John Rey. *Stone Fox.* (Harper and Row Junior Books, 1980)

Grahame, Kenneth. *The Wind in the Willows.* (Macmillan, 1989)

Howe, James. *Bunnicula: The Vampire Bunny and His Friends.* (Avon, 1986)

Howe, James. *Celery Stalks at Midnight.* (Macmillan, 1983)

Howe, James. *Howliday Inn.* (Avon, 1983)

Kjelgaard, Jim. *Big Red.* (Bantam, 1982)

Kjelgaard, Jim. *Outlaw Red.* (Bantam, 1977)

Knight, Eric. *Lassie, Come Home.* (Dell, 1989)

London, Jack. *Call of the Wild.* (Troll Associates, 1990)

Non-Fiction

Ayer, Elizabeth. *Canada.* (Rourke Corp., 1990)

Brazer, Marjorie C. *Well-Favored Passage: A Guide to Lake Huron's North Channel.* (Heron Books, 1987)

Broker, Ignatia. *Night Flying Woman: An Ojibway Narrative.* (Minnesota Historical Society Press, 1983)

Foster, Janet. *Working for Wildlife: The Beginning of Preservation in Canada.* (Books on Demand)

Johnston, Basil. *Ojibway Heritage.* (University of Nebraska Press, 1990)

Sabin, Lewis. *Canada.* (Troll Associates, 1985)

Stan, S. *The Ojibway.* (Rourke Corp., 1989)

Tanner, Helen H. *The Ojibway.* (Chelsea House, 1992)

Wright, David K. *Canada.* (Gareth Stevens Inc., 1991)

Answer Key

Page 10

1. Accept appropriate responses.

2. The animals are staying with John Longridge because the owners, the Hunters, are temporarily living in England.

3. The Labrador decides to go home to the Hunters.

4. The author means that there were very few humans inhabiting this part of the world.

5. The Labrador shook John's hand, the cat managed to knock John's note into the fire, and there was a bad phone connection when John spoke to Mrs. Oakes.

6. John didn't worry about the animals because they had never before wandered from the large garden area.

7. Mrs. Oakes found only part of the note John left and she knew he likes being with the animals.

8. The Labrador does not like to hunt for his own food, and the bull terrier is totally worn out after only one day.

9. The Labrador's instinct told him that the Hunter home was due west.

10. It was clear to the Labrador that he would make it home to the Hunters.

Page 15

1. Accept appropriate responses.

2. The Labrador made sure the old bull terrier walked on softer ground had more shade and food.

3. It was not in the Labrador's nature to kill living creatures for any reason.

4. The cub was curious about the bull terrier and scratched the dog's shoulder by pawing at him. The cat attacked the cub, enraging the mother bear. The cat's attack distracted the bear and her cub away from the bull terrier.

5. Helvi's family brought food for the bull terrier, and the other animals waited for several days before they tried to travel again.

6. It took the old dog three days.

7. The Ojibways gave them food and made them feel welcome.

8. The Labrador was anxious to continue the journey right away.

9. The Ojibways considered the bull terrier to be "the virtuous white dog of Omen."

10. The Ojibways believed the omen would prove fortunate because the bull terrier allowed the cat to steal some of his meat.

Page 11

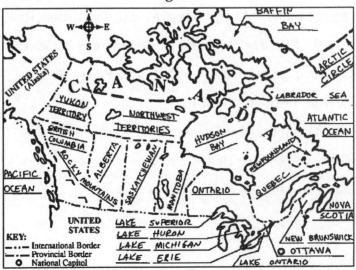

Answer Key (cont.)

Page 16

Top Graph:

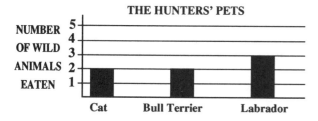

THE HUNTERS' PETS

Bottom Graph:

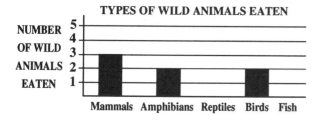

TYPES OF WILD ANIMALS EATEN

Page 20

1. Accept appropriate responses.
2. The Labrador is very hungry, but he does not feel comfortable hunting for his own food.
3. The old man treats them as if they are human.
4. The cat is swept many miles downstream.
5. Helvi is 10 years old and attends school. Her parents are Finnish immigrants who make their living by farming.
6. Reino Nurmi figures out that the cat is deaf because he does not respond when a bird flies overhead and when Reino clapped his hands near the cat's head.
7. The legend says that the princess took her cat with her when she went to bathe. The princess put her rings on the cat's tail for safe keeping. The cat bent her tail because she did not want to lose the rings.

8. The cat stays for 4 days.
9. Helvi realizes that the cat can hear and that it doesn't need her any more. The cat is the first friend she has had in a long time.
10. The cat is sneaking away from Helvi's house, and she is watching him go.

Page 25

1. Accept appropriate responses.
2. The old dog gave into liking Tao when he was a kitten because Tao was so feisty and the dog realized that they had something in common, their dislike for other cats.
3. The two dogs encounter a live porcupine and a farmer's black collie. They win the fight with the collie. But, the live porcupine fights back, and the Labrador ends up with quills in his cheek.
4. The cat buries his prey, walks carefully and lightly, and sleeps in the high branches of trees.
5. The cat is saved when a boy who is out hunting shoots the lynx.
6. The trio are wildly excited to see each other.
7. The trio have traveled 200 miles.
8. The bull terrier walks up to their door hoping for food.
9. Mr. Mackenzie takes the quills out of the Labrador's cheeks and Mrs. Mackenzie feeds the animals.
10. The last 50 miles of the trip will be the toughest part because of the terrain.

Page 30

1. Accept appropriate responses.
2. John is very depressed that the animals have left, and he doesn't know how to tell the Hunters.
3. The clues are the charred note, the timing of the animal's departure, and Luath shaking John's hand on the day that the animals leave.

Answer Key *(cont.)*

4. Mrs. Oakes fears that the animals must be dead, and she truly loves them.

5. John never liked the big dog sleeping on his bed. However, tonight he would have given the bed to the dog if he would just come back.

6. Peter is sure they will never make it home, and Elizabeth is sure that they will get home.

7. John goes to get away from the phone calls that never turn up any solid information on the trio, and he goes to help the Hunters celebrate Peter's birthday.

8. He remembers how frustrated he felt because Bodger was not a good hunting dog.

9. Peter is very excited and runs as fast as he can to Bodger to make up for the time they have missed being together.

10. The two are inseparable and have lived through so much together. They truly love one another.

Page 31

John Longridge goes on a trip, and the animals begin their journey.

The cat is washed downstream when the beaver dam breaks.

Helvi Nurmi rescues the cat from drowning.

The Labrador gets porcupine quills in his cheek.

The Labrador and the bull terrier encounter the collie.

The cat is almost eaten by a lynx.

The two dogs are reunited with the cat.

Mr. and Mrs. Mackenzie take care of the two dogs.

Page 42

Matching

1. Ojibways

2. Helvi Nurmi

3. John Longridge

4. Hunter Family

5. Mackenzies

True or False

1. False

2. True

3. True

4. False

5. False

Short Answers

1. Luath is being driven by his unconditional love for the Hunters.

2. The Labrador repeatedly showed them how they could swim across the river.

3. The first porcupine the Labrador had encountered was dead, and that was his only experience with a porcupine.

4. John retraced their steps on a map, and started calling people who might be able to help him in his search.

5. The cat loves the bull terrier so much that he wants them to complete the journey together.

Essays

1. Accept appropriate answers.

2. Accept appropriate answers.

Page 44

Perform the conversations for the class. Ask students to respond to the conversations in several different ways, such as, "Are the conversations realistic?" or "Are the words the characters say in keeping with their personalities?"

48